# The Egg Cookbook

60 Egg Recipes

**Copyright © 2023 by Himanshu Patel**

All rights reserved. No part of this publication may be reproduced, distributed, or transmitted in any form or by any means, including photocopying, recording, or other electronic or mechanical methods, without the prior written permission of the publisher, except in the case of brief quotations embodied in critical reviews and certain other noncommercial uses permitted by copyright law.

# Introduction: The Egg Cookbook 60 Egg Recipes

Welcome to the latest and tastiest edition of "The Egg Cookbook," where the incredible versatility of eggs takes center stage! Eggs have been a culinary cornerstone for centuries, loved for their simplicity, nutritional richness, and ability to transform into a myriad of delectable dishes. As we present this 2024 edition, we embark on a gastronomic journey that celebrates the incredible egg in all its glory.

In the culinary world, eggs are a symbol of endless possibilities, and this cookbook is a testament to their remarkable role in creating delightful breakfasts, satisfying lunches, and sumptuous dinners. Whether you're a seasoned chef or an enthusiastic home cook, you'll find inspiration on every page to elevate your egg-cooking skills to new heights.

Inside these pages, you'll discover 60 meticulously crafted egg recipes that span the culinary spectrum. From classic breakfast staples like perfectly poached eggs and fluffy omelets to innovative and globally inspired dishes that showcase the egg's incredible adaptability, there's something for every palate and occasion.

As we embrace the year 2024, we've curated this collection to reflect contemporary tastes and nutritional preferences. You'll find recipes that cater to various dietary needs, including vegetarian, keto-friendly, and protein-packed options. Whether you're looking for a quick and nutritious meal on a busy morning or aiming to impress guests with a sophisticated dinner, "The Egg Cookbook" has you covered.

Each recipe is a celebration of the egg's incredible ability to add richness, flavor, and nutrition to a wide range of dishes. We encourage you to explore, experiment, and savor the magic that eggs bring to the table. As you embark on this culinary adventure, may you discover new favorites, hone your culinary skills, and appreciate the humble egg in all its culinary glory.

# 1. Masala Omelette:

- Preparation Time: 10 minutes
- Cooking Time: 5 minutes

Ingredients:
- 2 eggs
- 1 onion, finely chopped
- 1 tomato, finely chopped
- 1 green chili, finely chopped
- 1/2 teaspoon turmeric powder
- Salt to taste
- 2 tablespoons oil

Instructions:
1. In a bowl, beat the eggs thoroughly.
2. Add chopped onion, tomato, green chili, turmeric powder, and a pinch of salt. Mix well.
3. Heat oil in a pan over medium heat.
4. Pour the egg mixture into the pan and let it cook until the edges are golden brown.
5. Flip the omelette and cook the other side until fully set.
6. Serve hot with toast or paratha.

## 2. Egg Curry:

- Preparation Time: 15 minutes
- Cooking Time: 20 minutes

Ingredients:
- 4 boiled eggs
- 1 onion, finely chopped
- 2 tomatoes, pureed
- 1 tablespoon ginger-garlic paste
- 1 teaspoon cumin powder
- 1 teaspoon coriander powder
- 1/2 teaspoon red chili powder
- 1/2 teaspoon turmeric powder
- Salt to taste
- Fresh coriander leaves for garnish

Instructions:
1. Heat oil in a pan, add chopped onions, and sauté until golden brown.
2. Add ginger-garlic paste and sauté for a minute until fragrant.
3. Pour in the tomato puree, cumin powder, coriander powder, red chili powder, turmeric powder, and salt. Cook until the oil separates.
4. Add the boiled eggs, coating them in the curry mixture.
5. Pour in some water, cover the pan, and simmer for 10 minutes.
6. Garnish with fresh coriander leaves and serve with rice or bread.

## 3. Egg Biryani:

- Preparation Time: 20 minutes
- Cooking Time: 30 minutes

Ingredients:
- 2 cups basmati rice, soaked
- 4 boiled eggs
- 1 onion, thinly sliced
- 1 tomato, chopped
- 1/4 cup yogurt
- 1/2 cup fried onions (for garnish)
- 1 teaspoon biryani masala
- 1/2 teaspoon turmeric powder
- 1/2 teaspoon red chili powder
- Fresh coriander and mint leaves for garnish

Instructions:
1. Cook the rice until 70% done and set aside.
2. In a pan, sauté sliced onions until golden brown.
3. Add chopped tomatoes, biryani masala, turmeric powder, and red chili powder. Cook until the tomatoes are soft.
4. Layer the half-cooked rice and boiled eggs in a pot, repeating the layers.
5. Garnish with fried onions, coriander, and mint leaves. Dum cook for 15 minutes.

## 4. Anda Bhurji (Spicy Scrambled Eggs):

- Preparation Time: 10 minutes
- Cooking Time: 10 minutes

Ingredients:
- 4 eggs
- 1 onion, finely chopped
- 1 tomato, chopped
- 1 green chili, chopped
- 1/2 teaspoon turmeric powder
- 1/2 teaspoon garam masala
- Salt to taste
- Fresh coriander leaves for garnish

Instructions:
1. Heat oil in a pan and sauté finely chopped onions until translucent.
2. Add chopped tomatoes, green chili, turmeric powder, garam masala, and a pinch of salt. Cook until the tomatoes are soft.
3. Beat the eggs and pour them into the pan. Stir continuously until fully cooked.
4. Garnish with fresh coriander leaves and serve with bread or chapati.

## 5. Egg Korma:

- Preparation Time: 15 minutes
- Cooking Time: 25 minutes

Ingredients:
- 4 boiled eggs
- 1 onion, finely sliced
- 1/2 cup coconut milk
- 1/2 cup yogurt
- 1 tablespoon ginger-garlic paste
- 1 teaspoon fennel seeds
- 1/2 teaspoon turmeric powder
- 1/2 teaspoon red chili powder
- Fresh coriander leaves for garnish

Instructions:
1. Heat oil in a pan, add finely sliced onions, and sauté until golden brown.
2. Add ginger-garlic paste and fennel seeds, sauté until aromatic.
3. Pour in coconut milk and yogurt, bringing it to a simmer.
4. Add boiled eggs, coat them with the curry, and cook for 10 minutes.
5. Garnish with fresh coriander leaves and serve with rice or naan.

## 6. Chinese Tea Leaf Eggs:

- Preparation Time: 15 minutes
- Cooking Time: 1-2 hours (marinating)

Ingredients:
- 6 hard-boiled eggs
- 2 tablespoons soy sauce
- 1 tablespoon black tea leaves
- 1 tablespoon sugar
- 1 cinnamon stick
- 2 star anise
- 1 teaspoon salt

Instructions:
1. Gently crack the boiled eggs' shells without peeling them.
2. In a pot, combine soy sauce, tea leaves, sugar, cinnamon stick, star anise, and salt.
3. Add the cracked eggs to the pot and fill with enough water to cover the eggs.
4. Simmer on low heat for 1-2 hours, allowing the flavors to infuse and the cracked patterns to form on the eggs.
5. Once done, peel the eggs and serve as a flavorful snack or appetizer.

## 7. Japanese Tamago Sushi :

- Preparation Time: 15 minutes
- Cooking Time: 5 minutes

Ingredients:
- 2 cups sushi rice, cooked and seasoned
- 4 eggs
- 2 tablespoons sugar
- 2 tablespoons soy sauce
- 1 tablespoon mirin (sweet rice wine)
- Nori sheets (seaweed)

Instructions:
1. In a bowl, whisk together eggs, sugar, soy sauce, and mirin.
2. Heat a non-stick pan over medium heat and pour in the egg mixture.
3. Cook, stirring gently, until the eggs are just set but still slightly runny.
4. Place a sheet of nori on a bamboo sushi mat, spread sushi rice evenly, and add a strip of the cooked egg.
5. Roll the sushi tightly, slice, and serve with soy sauce and pickled ginger.

## 8. Chinese Egg Drop Soup:

- Preparation Time: 10 minutes
- Cooking Time: 10 minutes

Ingredients:
- 4 cups chicken or vegetable broth
- 2 eggs, beaten
- 1 tablespoon cornstarch mixed with 2 tablespoons water
- 1 teaspoon soy sauce
- 1/2 teaspoon sesame oil
- Green onions, chopped, for garnish

Instructions:
1. In a pot, bring the broth to a simmer.
2. Stir in the cornstarch mixture to thicken the soup slightly.
3. Slowly pour beaten eggs into the simmering broth, stirring gently to create ribbons.
4. Add soy sauce and sesame oil, stir gently, and remove from heat.
5. Garnish with chopped green onions and serve hot.

## 9. Japanese Okonomiyaki:

- Preparation Time: 15 minutes
- Cooking Time: 15 minutes

Ingredients:
- 2 cups cabbage, finely shredded
- 1 cup all-purpose flour
- 2 eggs
- 3/4 cup dashi (Japanese broth)
- 2 tablespoons soy sauce
- 1/2 cup green onions, chopped
- 1/4 cup tenkasu (tempura scraps)
- Bonito flakes and okonomiyaki sauce for topping

Instructions:
1. In a bowl, mix shredded cabbage, flour, eggs, dashi, soy sauce, green onions, and tenkasu.
2. Heat a griddle or non-stick pan and pour the batter into a round shape.
3. Cook until the edges are golden, flip, and cook the other side.
4. Transfer to a plate, drizzle with okonomiyaki sauce, and sprinkle bonito flakes on top.
5. Slice and serve as a savory Japanese pancake.

## 10. Chinese Steamed Egg Custard:

- Preparation Time: 10 minutes
- Cooking Time: 15 minutes

Ingredients:
- 3 eggs
- 1 cup chicken or vegetable broth
- 1 tablespoon soy sauce
- 1/2 teaspoon sesame oil
- Green onions and cilantro for garnish

Instructions:
1. In a bowl, beat the eggs and mix in broth, soy sauce, and sesame oil.
2. Strain the mixture through a fine sieve into a heatproof dish.
3. Cover the dish with foil or a lid and place it in a steamer.
4. Steam for about 15 minutes or until the custard is set.
5. Garnish with chopped green onions and cilantro before serving.

## 11. Korean Gyeran Mari (계란말이):

- Preparation Time: 10 minutes
- Cooking Time: 5 minutes

Ingredients:
- 4 eggs
- Salt and pepper to taste
- 1 tablespoon vegetable oil
- 1/2 cup carrots, julienned
- 1/2 cup spinach, blanched and squeezed
- 1/2 cup bell peppers, thinly sliced
- 1/4 cup green onions, chopped

Instructions:
1. Beat the eggs in a bowl and season with salt and pepper.
2. Heat oil in a non-stick pan and pour a thin layer of beaten eggs.
3. Place carrots, spinach, bell peppers, and green onions on the egg.
4. Roll the egg tightly like a sushi roll. Repeat with the remaining ingredients.
5. Slice and serve the rolled omelette with soy sauce if desired.

## 12. Vietnamese Bánh Mì Trứng Opla (Egg Sandwich):

- Preparation Time: 10 minutes
- Cooking Time: 5 minutes

Ingredients:
- Baguette or bread rolls
- 2 eggs
- Butter for spreading
- Salt and pepper to taste
- Optional toppings: cilantro, pickled carrots and daikon, cucumber slices

Instructions:
1. Heat a pan and melt butter.
2. Crack the eggs into the pan, season with salt and pepper, and fry to your liking.
3. Split the baguette or bread rolls, spread with butter.
4. Place the fried eggs in the bread and add optional toppings.
5. Close the sandwich and enjoy your Vietnamese-style egg banh mi.

# 13. Korean Japchae (잡채) with Quail Eggs:

- Preparation Time: 20 minutes
- Cooking Time: 20 minutes

Ingredients:
- 200g sweet potato noodles (dangmyeon)
- 10 quail eggs
- 1 carrot, julienned
- 1 onion, thinly sliced
- 1/2 cup spinach, blanched and squeezed
- 2 tablespoons soy sauce
- 1 tablespoon sesame oil
- Sesame seeds for garnish

Instructions:
1. Cook sweet potato noodles according to package instructions, drain, and set aside.
2. Boil quail eggs for 5 minutes, peel, and set aside.
3. In a pan, sauté carrot and onion until tender.
4. Add spinach, cooked noodles, soy sauce, and sesame oil. Mix well.
5. Garnish with quail eggs and sesame seeds before serving.

## 14. Vietnamese Cơm Gà Xôi Mỡ (Chicken Sticky Rice with Egg):

- Preparation Time: 20 minutes
- Cooking Time: 30 minutes

Ingredients:
- 1 cup glutinous rice, soaked
- 200g chicken, cooked and shredded
- 2 eggs, fried into a thin omelette and sliced
- 2 Chinese sausages, sliced
- 2 tablespoons soy sauce
- Green onions and cilantro for garnish

Instructions:
1. Steam glutinous rice until cooked.
2. In a pan, sauté shredded chicken, Chinese sausages, and soy sauce.
3. Mix the cooked rice with the chicken mixture.
4. Top with sliced fried eggs, green onions, and cilantro.
5. Serve warm as a comforting Vietnamese dish.

## 15. Korean Gyeran Bokkeumbap (계란 볶음밥 - Egg Fried Rice):

- Preparation Time: 15 minutes
- Cooking Time: 10 minutes

Ingredients:
- 3 cups cooked rice, chilled
- 2 eggs, beaten
- 1 cup mixed vegetables (peas, carrots, corn)
- 1 cup cooked and shredded chicken (optional)
- 2 tablespoons soy sauce
- 1 tablespoon sesame oil
- Green onions for garnish

Instructions:
1. Heat a large pan or wok and scramble the beaten eggs.
2. Add mixed vegetables and cooked chicken, if using.
3. Stir in chilled rice and soy sauce, mixing well.
4. Drizzle with sesame oil and garnish with chopped green onions.
5. Serve hot as a quick and satisfying Korean fried rice.

## 16. Shakshuka - Gulf Style:

- Preparation Time: 15 minutes
- Cooking Time: 20 minutes

Ingredients:
- 4 eggs
- 1 onion, finely chopped
- 2 bell peppers, diced
- 3 tomatoes, chopped
- 2 cloves garlic, minced
- 1 teaspoon ground cumin
- 1 teaspoon paprika
- Salt and pepper to taste
- Fresh parsley for garnish

Instructions:
1. In a skillet, sauté onions and garlic until softened.
2. Add diced bell peppers and tomatoes. Cook until the tomatoes break down.
3. Season with cumin, paprika, salt, and pepper.
4. Create small wells in the mixture and crack eggs into them.
5. Cover and cook until the eggs are set. Garnish with fresh parsley.

## 17. Balaleet - Sweet Vermicelli with Eggs:

- Preparation Time: 15 minutes
- Cooking Time: 20 minutes

Ingredients:
- 1 cup vermicelli
- 4 eggs, beaten
- 1/4 cup sugar
- 1/2 teaspoon ground cardamom
- 2 tablespoons ghee
- Chopped nuts for garnish

Instructions:
1. Cook vermicelli according to package instructions, then drain.
2. In a pan, heat ghee and add vermicelli, stirring until golden.
3. Pour in beaten eggs, sugar, and cardamom. Mix until eggs are cooked.
4. Garnish with chopped nuts and serve warm as a sweet breakfast dish.

## 18. Harees - Wheat and Chicken Porridge:

- Preparation Time: 15 minutes
- Cooking Time: 2-3 hours (slow-cooked)

Ingredients:
- 1 cup wheat berries
- 1 cup shredded chicken
- 1 teaspoon ground cinnamon
- Salt to taste
- Ghee for drizzling

Instructions:
1. Rinse wheat berries and soak them overnight.
2. In a pot, combine soaked wheat, shredded chicken, and enough water.
3. Slow-cook for 2-3 hours, stirring occasionally until it reaches a porridge-like consistency.
4. Season with ground cinnamon and salt.
5. Drizzle with ghee before serving and enjoy this traditional Gulf dish.

## 19. Dangoor - Gulf-Style Scrambled Eggs:

- Preparation Time: 10 minutes
- Cooking Time: 10 minutes

Ingredients:
- 4 eggs
- 1 tomato, finely chopped
- 1 onion, finely chopped
- 2 green chilies, chopped
- 1/4 cup fresh coriander, chopped
- Salt and pepper to taste

Instructions:
1. In a bowl, beat the eggs and season with salt and pepper.
2. In a pan, sauté onions until golden, then add tomatoes and green chilies.
3. Pour the beaten eggs into the pan, stirring until fully cooked.
4. Garnish with fresh coriander and serve hot with bread or rice.

## 20. Mandi Rice with Eggs:

- Preparation Time: 30 minutes
- Cooking Time: 1 hour

Ingredients:
- 2 cups basmati rice
- 4 eggs
- 1/2 cup yogurt
- 1 onion, thinly sliced
- 1/4 cup raisins
- Whole spices (cardamom, cloves, cinnamon)
- Ghee for cooking

Instructions:
1. Rinse and soak basmati rice for 30 minutes.
2. In a pot, sauté sliced onions in ghee until golden.
3. Add whole spices and rice, stirring to coat.
4. Pour in yogurt and add enough water to cook the rice.
5. Halfway through cooking, create wells in the rice and crack eggs into them.
6. Cover and continue cooking until the rice and eggs are fully cooked.

## 21. Jareesh (جريش) with Eggs:

- Preparation Time: 15 minutes
- Cooking Time: 1-2 hours (for soaked wheat)

Ingredients:
- 1 cup jareesh (crushed wheat)
- 4 eggs
- 1 onion, finely chopped
- 2 cloves garlic, minced
- 1 teaspoon ground cumin
- Salt to taste
- Olive oil for cooking

Instructions:
1. Soak jareesh in water for a few hours or overnight.
2. In a pot, sauté chopped onions and garlic in olive oil until golden.
3. Add soaked jareesh, ground cumin, and salt. Cook until the wheat is tender.
4. Create wells in the jareesh and crack eggs into them.
5. Cover and cook until the eggs are set. Serve warm.

## 22. Khameer Bread with Eggs (خمير):

- Preparation Time: 30 minutes
- Cooking Time: 15 minutes

Ingredients:
- 2 cups all-purpose flour
- 1 tablespoon sugar
- 1 teaspoon instant yeast
- 1/2 cup warm milk
- 2 eggs
- Ghee for frying

Instructions:
1. Mix flour, sugar, yeast, warm milk, and one beaten egg to form a dough.
2. Knead the dough until smooth, then let it rise until doubled in size.
3. Divide the dough into small balls, flatten them, and make a small well in the center.
4. Crack an egg into the well and fry the bread in ghee until golden.
5. Serve warm as a delicious Gulf-style breakfast.

## 23. Qatayef (قطايف) - Stuffed Pancakes:

- Preparation Time: 30 minutes
- Cooking Time: 15 minutes

Ingredients:
- 2 cups qatayef mix (available in Middle Eastern stores)
- 1 cup ricotta cheese
- 1 cup chopped nuts (walnuts or pistachios)
- 1/2 cup sugar
- 1 teaspoon orange blossom water
- Ghee for frying

Instructions:
1. Prepare qatayef batter according to package instructions.
2. Heat a griddle, pour small circles of batter, and cook until bubbles form.
3. Mix ricotta cheese, chopped nuts, sugar, and orange blossom water for the filling.
4. Stuff each pancake with the filling and fold into a half-moon shape.
5. Fry the stuffed qatayef in ghee until golden. Drizzle with honey before serving.

## 24. Salona (سلونة) - Gulf-Style Egg and Vegetable Stew:

- Preparation Time: 20 minutes
- Cooking Time: 30 minutes

Ingredients:
- 4 eggs
- 1 cup okra, chopped
- 1 cup zucchini, diced
- 1 cup carrots, sliced
- 1 onion, finely chopped
- 2 tomatoes, chopped
- 2 tablespoons tomato paste
- 1 teaspoon ground coriander
- Salt and pepper to taste

Instructions:
1. In a pot, sauté chopped onions until translucent.
2. Add chopped tomatoes, tomato paste, and ground coriander. Cook until tomatoes are soft.
3. Add okra, zucchini, and carrots. Cook until vegetables are tender.
4. Create small wells in the stew and crack eggs into them. Cover until the eggs are cooked to your liking.
5. Season with salt and pepper. Serve the salona with rice or bread.

## 25. Luqaimat (لقيمات) - Sweet Dumplings with Eggs:

- Preparation Time: 20 minutes
- Cooking Time: 15 minutes

Ingredients:
- 2 cups all-purpose flour
- 1 teaspoon instant yeast
- 1 cup warm water
- 1/4 cup sugar
- 2 eggs
- Sesame seeds for garnish
- Date syrup or honey for drizzling

Instructions:
1. Mix flour, instant yeast, warm water, sugar, and one beaten egg to form a batter.
2. Let the batter rise for about 15 minutes.
3. Heat oil in a deep fryer or pan.
4. Scoop small portions of the batter and fry until golden.
5. Drizzle with date syrup or honey, sprinkle sesame seeds, and serve these sweet dumplings warm.

## 26. South African Bobotie:

- Preparation Time: 30 minutes
- Cooking Time: 45 minutes

Ingredients:
- 1 lb ground beef or lamb
- 1 onion, finely chopped
- 2 slices bread, soaked in milk
- 2 tablespoons curry powder
- 1 tablespoon apricot jam
- 1 tablespoon vinegar
- 2 eggs
- Bay leaves for garnish

Instructions:
1. Preheat the oven to 350°F (180°C).
2. Sauté chopped onions until golden, then add ground meat and cook until browned.
3. Mix in soaked bread, curry powder, apricot jam, and vinegar.
4. Transfer the mixture to a baking dish and smooth the top.
5. Beat eggs and pour over the meat, placing bay leaves on top.
6. Bake for 45 minutes or until the egg topping is set and golden.

## 27. Nigerian Jollof Rice with Fried Eggs:

- Preparation Time: 30 minutes
- Cooking Time: 40 minutes

Ingredients:
- 2 cups parboiled rice
- 1 cup tomato puree
- 1 onion, diced
- 2 red bell peppers, chopped
- 2 cups chicken or vegetable broth
- 4 eggs, fried
- Vegetable oil for frying
- Jollof rice seasoning (thyme, curry powder, bay leaves)

Instructions:
1. In a pot, sauté diced onions in vegetable oil until translucent.
2. Add chopped red bell peppers and cook until softened.
3. Stir in tomato puree, jollof rice seasoning, and parboiled rice. Mix well.
4. Pour in broth, cover, and simmer until the rice is cooked.
5. Fry eggs separately and serve them on top of the Jollof rice.

## 28. Ethiopian Doro Wat (Spicy Chicken Stew):

- Preparation Time: 30 minutes
- Cooking Time: 1 hour

Ingredients:
- 1 whole chicken, cut into pieces
- 2 large onions, finely chopped
- 4 cloves garlic, minced
- 1 tablespoon ginger, grated
- 1/4 cup berbere spice
- 2 tablespoons tomato paste
- 4 hard-boiled eggs
- Vegetable oil
- Injera (Ethiopian flatbread) for serving

Instructions:
1. Sauté chopped onions in vegetable oil until golden.
2. Add minced garlic, grated ginger, berbere spice, and tomato paste. Cook until fragrant.
3. Add chicken pieces, coating them in the spice mixture.
4. Pour in enough water to cover the chicken and simmer until cooked.
5. Add hard-boiled eggs and serve the Doro Wat with injera.

## 29. Ghanaian Kelewele (Spicy Fried Plantains):

- Preparation Time: 15 minutes
- Cooking Time: 10 minutes

Ingredients:
- 4 ripe plantains, peeled and sliced
- 1 tablespoon ginger, grated
- 1 teaspoon cayenne pepper
- 1 teaspoon ground cinnamon
- Salt to taste
- Vegetable oil for frying
- Fried eggs for serving

Instructions:
1. In a bowl, mix grated ginger, cayenne pepper, ground cinnamon, and salt.
2. Toss the plantain slices in the spice mixture until well coated.
3. Heat vegetable oil in a pan and fry the plantains until golden brown.
4. Serve Kelewele with fried eggs for a delightful Ghanaian snack.

# 30. Moroccan Shakshuka with Merguez Sausage:

- Preparation Time: 20 minutes
- Cooking Time: 25 minutes

Ingredients:
- 4 eggs
- 1 onion, finely chopped
- 2 bell peppers, diced
- 2 cloves garlic, minced
- 4 Merguez sausages, sliced
- 2 cans (400g each) diced tomatoes
- 1 teaspoon cumin
- 1 teaspoon paprika
- Fresh cilantro for garnish
- Crusty bread for serving

Instructions:
1. In a skillet, sauté chopped onions, bell peppers, and garlic until softened.
2. Add sliced Merguez sausage and cook until browned.
3. Pour in diced tomatoes and season with cumin and paprika.
4. Create wells in the tomato mixture and crack eggs into them.
5. Cover and cook until the eggs are set. Garnish with fresh cilantro.
6. Serve the Shakshuka with crusty bread for a hearty Moroccan meal.

## 31. Tunisian Ojja (Spicy Seafood and Egg Stew):

- Preparation Time: 20 minutes
- Cooking Time: 30 minutes

Ingredients:
- 1 lb mixed seafood (shrimp, mussels, calamari)
- 4 eggs
- 1 onion, finely chopped
- 2 bell peppers, sliced
- 3 tomatoes, diced
- 3 cloves garlic, minced
- 1 teaspoon harissa paste
- 1 teaspoon ground cumin
- Fresh parsley for garnish

Instructions:
1. In a skillet, sauté chopped onions and garlic until golden.
2. Add sliced bell peppers, diced tomatoes, and harissa paste. Cook until tomatoes break down.
3. Add mixed seafood and ground cumin. Cook until the seafood is done.
4. Create wells in the mixture and crack eggs into them. Cover until the eggs are set.
5. Garnish with fresh parsley and serve.

## 32. Kenyan Sukuma Wiki with Eggs:

- Preparation Time: 20 minutes
- Cooking Time: 15 minutes

Ingredients:
- 2 bunches sukuma wiki (collard greens), chopped
- 4 eggs
- 1 onion, finely chopped
- 2 tomatoes, diced
- 2 tablespoons vegetable oil
- 1 teaspoon curry powder
- Salt and pepper to taste

Instructions:

1. In a pan, sauté chopped onions in vegetable oil until translucent.
2. Add diced tomatoes, curry powder, and chopped sukuma wiki. Cook until greens are wilted.
3. Create wells in the mixture and crack eggs into them. Cover until the eggs are set.
4. Season with salt and pepper before serving.

## 33. Moroccan Msemen (Square Flatbread) with Eggs:

- Preparation Time: 45 minutes
- Cooking Time: 15 minutes

Ingredients:
- 2 cups semolina flour
- 1 cup all-purpose flour
- 1 teaspoon sugar
- 1 teaspoon salt
- 1 cup warm water
- 1/2 cup vegetable oil
- 4 eggs
- Honey for drizzling

Instructions:
1. Mix semolina flour, all-purpose flour, sugar, and salt in a bowl.
2. Gradually add warm water, kneading to form a smooth dough.
3. Divide the dough into balls and let them rest for 30 minutes.
4. Roll out each ball into a square, brushing with vegetable oil.
5. Fold the squares into layers, then cook on a griddle until golden.
6. Fry eggs and serve them on top of Msemen with a drizzle of honey.

## 34. Scotch Woodcock (British Deviled Eggs):

- Preparation Time: 15 minutes
- Cooking Time: 10 minutes

Ingredients:
- 4 hard-boiled eggs, sliced
- 4 slices toast
- 4 tablespoons anchovy paste
- 4 tablespoons butter
- 4 tablespoons milk
- Salt and pepper to taste
- Chopped chives for garnish

Instructions:
1. Toast slices of bread and place them on a serving plate.
2. In a pan, melt butter and add anchovy paste, stirring until combined.
3. Add milk, salt, and pepper, and continue stirring until smooth.
4. Place sliced hard-boiled eggs on the toast and pour the anchovy mixture over them.
5. Garnish with chopped chives and serve the Scotch Woodcock.

## 35. Swiss Rösti with Fried Egg:

- Preparation Time: 20 minutes
- Cooking Time: 30 minutes

Ingredients:
- 4 large potatoes, peeled and grated
- 1 onion, finely chopped
- 4 eggs
- Butter for cooking
- Salt and pepper to taste

Instructions:
1. Mix grated potatoes with chopped onions.
2. In a skillet, melt butter and spread half of the potato mixture evenly.
3. Cook until the bottom is golden, then flip and cook the other side.
4. Repeat with the remaining potato mixture.
5. Fry eggs and place one on top of each rösti.
6. Season with salt and pepper and serve the Swiss rösti.

## 36. Mexican Chilaquiles Verdes:

- Preparation Time: 20 minutes
- Cooking Time: 15 minutes

Ingredients:
- 1 bag tortilla chips
- 1 cup salsa verde
- 1 cup cooked shredded chicken
- 1/2 cup crumbled queso fresco
- 4 eggs
- Fresh cilantro for garnish
- Avocado slices for serving

Instructions:
1. In a pan, heat salsa verde and add tortilla chips, tossing until coated.
2. Mix in shredded chicken and cook until heated through.
3. Create wells in the mixture and crack eggs into them. Cover until the eggs are set.
4. Sprinkle crumbled queso fresco and garnish with fresh cilantro.
5. Serve Chilaquiles Verdes with avocado slices.

## 37. Argentinian Tortilla Española:

- Preparation Time: 20 minutes
- Cooking Time: 25 minutes

Ingredients:
- 4 potatoes, thinly sliced
- 1 onion, thinly sliced
- 6 eggs
- Olive oil
- Salt and pepper to taste

Instructions:
1. In a pan, sauté sliced potatoes and onions in olive oil until tender.
2. Beat eggs in a bowl, season with salt and pepper.
3. Mix the eggs with the sautéed potatoes and onions.
4. In the same pan, pour the mixture and cook until set on the bottom.
5. Flip the tortilla and cook the other side until golden.

## 38. Peruvian Aji de Gallina:

- Preparation Time: 30 minutes
- Cooking Time: 30 minutes

Ingredients:
- 2 cups shredded cooked chicken
- 2 slices bread, soaked in milk
- 1 onion, chopped
- 2 yellow chili peppers, seeds removed and blended
- 2 cloves garlic, minced
- 1/2 cup grated Parmesan cheese
- 4 eggs, hard-boiled
- Black olives for garnish

Instructions:
1. Sauté chopped onions and minced garlic until softened.
2. Add blended yellow chili peppers and soaked bread. Cook until it forms a thick sauce.
3. Mix in shredded chicken and grated Parmesan cheese.
4. Pour the aji de gallina sauce over boiled eggs.
5. Garnish with black olives and serve with rice.

## 39. Brazilian Pão de Queijo (Cheese Bread) with Eggs:

- Preparation Time: 20 minutes
- Cooking Time: 15 minutes

Ingredients:
- 2 cups tapioca flour
- 1 cup milk
- 1/2 cup butter
- 1 teaspoon salt
- 2 cups grated Parmesan cheese
- 2 eggs

Instructions:
1. In a saucepan, heat milk, butter, and salt until it simmers.
2. Pour the hot milk mixture over tapioca flour, stirring until combined.
3. Let it cool slightly, then mix in grated Parmesan cheese and eggs.
4. Form small balls and bake until golden and puffy.
5. Serve Pão de Queijo with eggs for a delightful Brazilian breakfast.

# 40. Colombian Arepas Rellenas de Huevo (Stuffed Corn Cakes):

- Preparation Time: 30 minutes
- Cooking Time: 20 minutes

Ingredients:
- 2 cups masarepa (pre-cooked cornmeal)
- 2 1/2 cups warm water
- Salt to taste
- 4 eggs
- 1 cup shredded cheese (queso fresco or mozzarella)
- Vegetable oil for frying

Instructions:
1. Mix masarepa with warm water and salt to form a dough.
2. Divide the dough into balls and flatten them into discs.
3. Crack an egg into the center of each disc and sprinkle with shredded cheese.
4. Fold the edges over the egg and cheese, sealing the edges.
5. Fry the stuffed arepas until golden and the eggs are cooked.

## 41. Chilean Humitas:

- Preparation Time: 30 minutes
- Cooking Time: 1 hour

Ingredients:
- 6 fresh corn ears, kernels removed
- 1 cup cornmeal
- 1/2 cup butter
- 1 onion, finely chopped
- 1 teaspoon paprika
- 4 eggs
- 1/2 cup milk
- Salt and pepper to taste

Instructions:
1. In a blender, process corn kernels until smooth.
2. In a pan, sauté chopped onions in butter until golden.
3. Add processed corn, cornmeal, paprika, salt, and pepper. Cook until thickened.
4. In a bowl, beat eggs and mix with milk. Add to the corn mixture and cook until set.
5. Serve humitas warm, either as a main dish or side.

## 42. Puerto Rican Mofongo with Fried Egg:

- Preparation Time: 20 minutes
- Cooking Time: 15 minutes

Ingredients:
- 4 green plantains, peeled and sliced
- 1/2 cup pork rinds (chicharrones)
- 4 cloves garlic, minced
- 1/2 cup olive oil
- 4 eggs
- Salt and pepper to taste

Instructions:
1. Boil plantain slices until tender, then mash with minced garlic and chicharrones.
2. Form the mashed plantains into balls or a mound.
3. In a pan, heat olive oil and fry the plantain mixture until golden.
4. Create a well in the center and crack an egg into it. Cook until the egg is fried.
5. Serve Mofongo with a fried egg on top.

## 43. Ecuadorian Ceviche de Camarones (Shrimp Ceviche):

- Preparation Time: 30 minutes
- Cooking Time: 0 minutes (since it's a ceviche)

Ingredients:
- 1 lb shrimp, peeled and deveined
- 1 red onion, thinly sliced
- 2 tomatoes, diced
- 1 bell pepper, diced
- 1/2 cup cilantro, chopped
- 4 eggs
- Lime juice
- Salt and pepper to taste

Instructions:
1. Boil shrimp briefly in salted water until just cooked, then cool.
2. In a bowl, mix shrimp with sliced red onion, diced tomatoes, diced bell pepper, and chopped cilantro.
3. Squeeze lime juice over the mixture and season with salt and pepper.
4. Serve the shrimp ceviche with hard-boiled eggs on the side.

## 44. Guatemalan Hilachas:

- Preparation Time: 30 minutes
- Cooking Time: 2 hours

Ingredients:
- 2 lbs beef, shredded
- 1 onion, finely chopped
- 3 tomatoes, diced
- 2 carrots, sliced
- 1/2 cup green beans, chopped
- 4 eggs
- 4 potatoes, boiled and sliced
- 1/2 cup pumpkin seeds (pepitas), toasted
- Cilantro for garnish

Instructions:
1. In a pot, cook shredded beef with chopped onions, diced tomatoes, sliced carrots, and chopped green beans.
2. Add boiled and sliced potatoes to the pot.
3. In a separate pan, fry eggs.
4. Serve Hilachas with a fried egg on top and garnish with toasted pumpkin seeds and cilantro.

## 45. Uruguayan Chivito Sandwich:

- Preparation Time: 20 minutes
- Cooking Time: 10 minutes

Ingredients:
- 4 beef tenderloin steaks
- 4 eggs
- 4 slices ham
- 4 slices bacon
- 4 slices mozzarella cheese
- Lettuce, tomatoes, and mayonnaise for garnish
- Bread rolls

Instructions:
1. Grill beef tenderloin steaks to desired doneness.
2. In a pan, fry eggs, bacon, and ham slices.
3. Assemble the Chivito sandwich with grilled steak, fried eggs, bacon, ham, mozzarella cheese, lettuce, tomatoes, and mayonnaise.
4. Serve the Chivito sandwich on a bread roll.

## 46. Cuban Ropa Vieja Omelette:

- Preparation Time: 15 minutes
- Cooking Time: 15 minutes

Ingredients:
- 1 cup shredded Ropa Vieja (shredded beef in tomato sauce)
- 4 eggs
- 1/2 cup bell peppers, diced
- 1/4 cup onions, finely chopped
- 1/4 cup tomatoes, diced
- 1/2 cup shredded cheese (cheddar or Monterey Jack)
- Salt and pepper to taste

Instructions:
1. In a bowl, beat eggs and season with salt and pepper.
2. Heat a skillet, add Ropa Vieja, bell peppers, onions, and tomatoes.
3. Pour the beaten eggs over the mixture and cook until set.
4. Sprinkle shredded cheese on top and fold the omelette before serving.

## 47. Venezuelan Arepa Reina Pepiada:

- Preparation Time: 30 minutes
- Cooking Time: 20 minutes

Ingredients:
- 2 cups pre-cooked corn flour (masarepa)
- 2 1/2 cups warm water
- 1 teaspoon salt
- 1 avocado, mashed
- 1 cup shredded chicken (pollo mechado)
- 4 hard-boiled eggs, sliced
- Mayonnaise for garnish

Instructions:
1. Mix masarepa with warm water and salt to form a smooth dough.
2. Shape the dough into small discs and cook until golden.
3. Slice the arepas and fill them with mashed avocado, shredded chicken, sliced hard-boiled eggs, and a dollop of mayonnaise.
4. Serve the Reina Pepiada arepas as a delightful Venezuelan snack.

## 48. Panamanian Torta de Huevo (Egg Frittata):

- Preparation Time: 20 minutes
- Cooking Time: 25 minutes

Ingredients:
- 6 eggs
- 1/2 cup cooked chorizo, crumbled
- 1/4 cup red bell pepper, diced
- 1/4 cup green bell pepper, diced
- 1/4 cup onion, finely chopped
- 1/2 cup queso blanco, crumbled (white cheese)
- Salt and pepper to taste

Instructions:
1. In a bowl, beat eggs and season with salt and pepper.
2. In a skillet, sauté chorizo, red and green bell peppers, and onions until softened.
3. Pour the beaten eggs over the mixture, sprinkle crumbled queso blanco, and cook until set.
4. Serve the Torta de Huevo as a delicious Panamanian frittata.

## 49. American Classic Eggs Benedict:

- Preparation Time: 15 minutes
- Cooking Time: 10 minutes

Ingredients:
- 4 English muffins, split and toasted
- 8 slices Canadian bacon
- 8 poached eggs
- Hollandaise sauce
- Chopped chives for garnish

Instructions:
1. Place a slice of Canadian bacon on each half of the toasted English muffins.
2. Top each with a poached egg.
3. Drizzle hollandaise sauce over the eggs.
4. Garnish with chopped chives.
5. Serve Eggs Benedict for a classic American breakfast.

## 50. Southern Style Deviled Eggs:

- Preparation Time: 20 minutes
- Cooking Time: 10 minutes (for boiling eggs)

Ingredients:
- 6 hard-boiled eggs
- 1/4 cup mayonnaise
- 1 tablespoon yellow mustard
- 1 teaspoon white vinegar
- Salt and pepper to taste
- Paprika for garnish

Instructions:
1. Cut hard-boiled eggs in half and remove yolks.
2. Mash yolks and mix with mayonnaise, yellow mustard, white vinegar, salt, and pepper.
3. Spoon or pipe the yolk mixture back into the egg whites.
4. Sprinkle paprika on top for garnish.
5. Serve Southern-style deviled eggs as a classic American appetizer.

## 51. Tex-Mex Breakfast Burrito:

- Preparation Time: 15 minutes
- Cooking Time: 10 minutes

Ingredients:
- 4 large flour tortillas
- 8 eggs, scrambled
- 1 cup cooked and seasoned ground sausage or chorizo
- 1 cup shredded cheddar cheese
- Salsa and sour cream for serving

Instructions:
1. In a skillet, cook scrambled eggs and seasoned ground sausage or chorizo.
2. Warm flour tortillas and fill each with a portion of the egg and sausage mixture.
3. Sprinkle shredded cheddar cheese on top.
4. Roll the tortillas into burritos.
5. Serve Tex-Mex breakfast burritos with salsa and sour cream.

## 52. Canadian Maple Bacon Pancake Stack:

- Preparation Time: 20 minutes
- Cooking Time: 15 minutes

Ingredients:
- Pancake mix (follow package instructions)
- 8 slices Canadian bacon
- Maple syrup
- Butter for cooking pancakes
- Whipped cream for garnish

Instructions:
1. Prepare pancake batter according to the package instructions.
2. Cook pancakes on a griddle with a bit of butter.
3. In a separate pan, cook Canadian bacon until crispy.
4. Stack pancakes with layers of Canadian bacon between them.
5. Drizzle with maple syrup and garnish with whipped cream.

## 53. American Diner-style Western Omelette:

- Preparation Time: 15 minutes
- Cooking Time: 10 minutes

Ingredients:
- 4 eggs
- 1/2 cup diced cooked ham
- 1/4 cup diced green bell pepper
- 1/4 cup diced onion
- 1/4 cup shredded cheddar cheese
- Salt and pepper to taste

Instructions:
1. In a bowl, beat eggs and season with salt and pepper.
2. In a skillet, sauté diced ham, green bell pepper, and onion until softened.
3. Pour beaten eggs over the sautéed mixture.
4. Sprinkle shredded cheddar cheese on top and fold the omelette.
5. Serve the Western omelette with toast for a classic American diner breakfast.

## 54. Italian Frittata with Spinach and Feta:

- Preparation Time: 15 minutes
- Cooking Time: 15 minutes

Ingredients:
- 6 eggs
- 1 cup fresh spinach, chopped
- 1/2 cup feta cheese, crumbled
- 1/4 cup grated Parmesan cheese
- 1 small onion, finely chopped
- Salt and pepper to taste

Instructions:
1. In a bowl, beat eggs and season with salt and pepper.
2. Sauté chopped onions in an oven-safe skillet until translucent.
3. Add chopped spinach and cook until wilted.
4. Pour beaten eggs over the spinach and onion mixture.
5. Sprinkle feta and Parmesan cheese on top.
6. Bake in the oven until the frittata is set and golden.

## 55. French Croque Madame:

- Preparation Time: 15 minutes
- Cooking Time: 10 minutes

Ingredients:
- 4 slices of bread
- 4 slices ham
- 4 slices Gruyère or Swiss cheese
- 4 eggs
- Butter for spreading
- Bechamel sauce (optional)
- Salt and pepper to taste

Instructions:
1. Spread butter on one side of each bread slice.
2. Place a slice of ham and cheese on two slices of bread.
3. Top each with another slice of bread, butter side up.
4. Grill the sandwiches until the bread is golden and the cheese is melted.
5. Fry or poach eggs and place one on top of each sandwich.
6. Optionally, drizzle with bechamel sauce and season with salt and pepper.

## 56. Spanish Tortilla Española:

- Preparation Time: 20 minutes
- Cooking Time: 20 minutes

Ingredients:
- 4 large potatoes, thinly sliced
- 1 onion, thinly sliced
- 6 eggs
- Olive oil
- Salt to taste

Instructions:
1. In a skillet, heat olive oil and fry potato and onion slices until tender.
2. Beat eggs in a bowl and season with salt.
3. Mix the eggs with the fried potatoes and onions.
4. In the same skillet, pour the mixture and cook until set on the bottom.
5. Flip the tortilla and cook the other side until golden.

## 57. Greek Spanakopita (Spinach Pie) with Eggs:

- Preparation Time: 30 minutes
- Cooking Time: 45 minutes

Ingredients:
- 1 package phyllo dough
- 1 lb fresh spinach, chopped
- 1 cup feta cheese, crumbled
- 4 eggs
- 1 onion, finely chopped
- Olive oil
- Salt and pepper to taste

Instructions:
1. Sauté chopped onions in olive oil until translucent.
2. Add chopped spinach and cook until wilted.
3. In a bowl, beat eggs and mix with feta cheese, salt, and pepper.
4. Layer phyllo dough in a baking dish, brushing each layer with olive oil.
5. Spread the spinach mixture over the phyllo layers.
6. Pour the egg and feta mixture over the spinach.
7. Bake until the phyllo is golden and the filling is set.

## 58. English Scotch Eggs:

- Preparation Time: 20 minutes
- Cooking Time: 15 minutes

Ingredients:
- 4 hard-boiled eggs
- 1 lb sausage meat
- 1 cup breadcrumbs
- 2 eggs, beaten
- Flour for coating
- Vegetable oil for frying

Instructions:
1. Peel the hard-boiled eggs.
2. Divide the sausage meat into four portions.
3. Flatten each portion and wrap around a hard-boiled egg.
4. Roll each sausage-covered egg in flour, then dip in beaten eggs and coat with breadcrumbs.
5. Fry in hot oil until golden and crispy.

## 59. German Bauernfrühstück (Farmers' Breakfast):

- Preparation Time: 20 minutes
- Cooking Time: 15 minutes

Ingredients:
- 4 potatoes, peeled and grated
- 1 onion, finely chopped
- 4 eggs
- 1/2 cup cooked ham, diced
- Salt and pepper to taste
- Butter for cooking

Instructions:
1. In a pan, sauté chopped onions in butter until translucent.
2. Add grated potatoes and cook until they start to brown.
3. Stir in diced ham.
4. Create wells in the potato mixture and crack eggs into them.
5. Cook until the eggs are set, season with salt and pepper.

## 60. Swedish Gravad Lax Eggs Benedict:

- Preparation Time: 15 minutes (plus curing time for gravad lax)
- Cooking Time: 10 minutes

Ingredients:
- 4 English muffins, split and toasted
- 8 slices gravad lax (cured salmon)
- 8 poached eggs
- Hollandaise sauce
- Fresh dill for garnish

Instructions:
1. Place a slice of gravad lax on each half of the toasted English muffins.
2. Top each with a poached egg.
3. Drizzle hollandaise sauce over the eggs.
4. Garnish with fresh dill.
5. Serve Gravad Lax Eggs Benedict for a Scandinavian twist.

**SCAN ME**

**free 65 chicken RECIPES cookbook inside**

*only in paperback

## 61. Portuguese Pastéis de Bacalhau (Codfish Fritters):

- Preparation Time: 30 minutes
- Cooking Time: 15 minutes

Ingredients:
- 2 cups salted codfish, boiled and shredded
- 4 potatoes, boiled and mashed
- 1 onion, finely chopped
- 2 cloves garlic, minced
- 2 eggs
- Fresh parsley, chopped
- Salt and pepper to taste

Instructions:
1. In a bowl, mix shredded codfish, mashed potatoes, chopped onions, minced garlic, and chopped parsley.
2. Beat eggs and add them to the mixture. Season with salt and pepper.
3. Form the mixture into small patties and fry until golden.
4. Serve Pastéis de Bacalhau with a side of aioli or tomato sauce.

## 62. Norwegian Koldtbord Eggs:

- Preparation Time: 20 minutes
- Cooking Time: 0 minutes (since it's a cold dish)

Ingredients:
- 4 hard-boiled eggs, sliced
- Smoked salmon slices
- Pickled herring
- Cream cheese
- Capers
- Rye bread

Instructions:
1. Arrange slices of smoked salmon on a serving platter.
2. Place slices of hard-boiled eggs on top.
3. Add pickled herring, dollops of cream cheese, and capers.
4. Serve the Koldtbord Eggs with slices of rye bread.

## 63. Spanish Huevos a la Flamenca:

- Preparation Time: 30 minutes

- Cooking Time: 20 minutes

Ingredients:
- 4 eggs
- 1 onion, finely chopped
- 2 bell peppers, diced
- 2 tomatoes, diced
- 1 chorizo sausage, sliced
- 1 cup cooked peas
- Paprika, cayenne pepper, salt, and pepper to taste

Instructions:
1. In a pan, sauté chopped onions until translucent.
2. Add diced bell peppers, tomatoes, and sliced chorizo. Cook until vegetables are softened.
3. Stir in cooked peas and season with paprika, cayenne pepper, salt, and pepper.
4. Create wells in the mixture and crack eggs into them.
5. Bake until the eggs are set, and the dish is bubbling.

## 64. French Quiche Lorraine:
- Preparation Time: 30 minutes
- Cooking Time: 40 minutes

Ingredients:
- 1 pie crust (store-bought or homemade)
- 1 cup bacon, cooked and chopped
- 1 cup Gruyère cheese, shredded
- 4 eggs
- 1 cup heavy cream
- Salt, pepper, and nutmeg to taste

Instructions:
1. Preheat the oven to 375°F (190°C).
2. In a pre-baked pie crust, layer bacon and Gruyère cheese.
3. In a bowl, whisk together eggs, heavy cream, salt, pepper, and nutmeg.
4. Pour the egg mixture over the bacon and cheese.
5. Bake until the quiche is set and golden brown.

## 65. Italian Caprese Omelette:
- Preparation Time: 15 minutes

- Cooking Time: 10 minutes

Ingredients:
- 4 eggs
- 1 cup cherry tomatoes, halved
- 1/2 cup fresh mozzarella, diced
- Fresh basil leaves, torn
- Olive oil
- Salt and pepper to taste

Instructions:
1. In a bowl, beat eggs and season with salt and pepper.
2. Heat olive oil in a skillet and pour in the beaten eggs.
3. Once the edges set, add cherry tomatoes, mozzarella, and torn basil leaves.
4. Fold the omelette and cook until the cheese melts.
5. Serve the Caprese omelette for a taste of Italy.

## 66. Dutch Poffertjes with Lemon and Powdered Sugar:

- Preparation Time: 15 minutes
- Cooking Time: 10 minutes

Ingredients:
- 1 cup poffertjes mix (or pancake mix)
- 1 cup milk
- Butter for cooking
- Lemon wedges
- Powdered sugar

Instructions:
1. Prepare poffertjes batter by mixing poffertjes mix with milk.
2. Heat a poffertjes pan and grease with butter.
3. Pour small amounts of batter into each dimple of the pan.
4. Cook until bubbles form, then flip and cook the other side.
5. Serve poffertjes with lemon wedges and a sprinkle of powdered sugar.

Printed in Great Britain
by Amazon

36746354R00040